Let freedom Ring!

Mertta Strandberg

Hey Kids, Want Some Chocolates?

My Family's Journey to Freedom

Melitta Strandberg

AuthorHouse™
1663 Liberty Drive
Bloomington, IN 47403
www.authorhouse.com
Phone: 1-800-839-8640

© 2011 Melitta Strandberg. All rights reserved.

No part of this book may be reproduced, stored in a retrieval system, or transmitted by any means without the written permission of the author.

First published by AuthorHouse 1/12/2011

ISBN: 978-1-4567-1793-3 (sc)
ISBN: 978-1-4567-1794-0 (e)

Library of Congress Control Number: 2011900067

Printed in the United States of America

This book is printed on acid-free paper.

Because of the dynamic nature of the Internet, any Web addresses or links contained in this book may have changed since publication and may no longer be valid. The views expressed in this work are solely those of the author and do not necessarily reflect the views of the publisher, and the publisher hereby disclaims any responsibility for them.

Dedication and Acknowledgments

This book is dedicated to my parents, Oskar Mohr and Gisela Csek Mohr. Without their brave and courageous quest to find freedom, my sister, brothers and I would probably have spent many years behind the Iron Curtain without freedom.

There are others that I would like to acknowledge. My sister, Grete Mohr Chastain, was born in 1939 and went through the horrible ordeals of war at an early age. She has conducted speaking engagements regarding her experiences, in her church and social groups in the Pacific Northwest. My brother, Wilhelm Mohr, who also heard the bombs in the first four years of his life, now lives in St. Petersburg, Florida. My younger brother, Alexander Mohr was born in Augsburg, Germany in 1954, and is now a successful businessman in Germany. After reaching freedom, my siblings and I lived normal and happy lives. But, we will never forget the early childhood years described in this book.

Last, but not least, I thank my husband, Herb, for supporting my goal of writing this book. Without him, I would not have had the courage to put my story into words.

Table of Contents

Foreword	ix
Introduction	xi
1 – Life Before the Journey	1
2 – The First Phase of Our Journey	9
3 – Life in Weimar, Germany	13
4 – Sept 3, 1944 And Subsequent Events	17
5 – The Last Year in Weimar	25
6 – The Journey to the West	29
7 – Freedom	37
8 – Life in Augsburg	45
9 – July 4, 1963	57
10 – A Life of Freedom and Faith in God	61

Foreword

In early June of 2010, I received an e-mail from Melitta Strandberg. The e-mail stated that she had a story regarding World War II and wondered if I would be interested in helping her write a book about the story. She indicated that she had a friend who was an acquaintance of mine from the early years of my life and who knew that I was an author.

At that time I had just published a book and had two other manuscripts in process so I did not answer, because there was plenty of work ahead for me without taking on another book. A couple of weeks later she again contacted me and attached a copy of her story. Finally, a few days later after another e-mail, I began reading her story. The more I read the more I became convinced that her story deserved publication. After a few more e-mail exchanges I agreed to co-author her story.

The part of the book that initially convinced me to help Melitta was the chapter of the events surrounding her birth. I have visited Dachau and have also heard the horrible stories of the human experiments that occurred under the Nazi regime, but had never met anyone who experienced it. Here was someone who was subjected to it from the first day of her life. That part of her life was enough to convince me to work with Melitta. I put my other projects on hold and began working with her.

However, that was only part of the story. Her parents' journey to find freedom is also a compelling story by itself. The more Melitta told me of her story the more intrigued I became with the experiences her family endured. In the comfortable country we live in today, it is easy to take freedom, that inalienable right given to us by our Creator, for granted. Melitta's family members did not have that luxury for many years of their lives. Her story as presented in this book should be a lesson to every American that freedom is a right which should never be taken for granted and deserves our perpetual vigilance.

Shortly after we began work on the book, my wife and I visited Melitta and her husband, Herb. It would be understandable that someone who did not see her parents for six months after her birth might be somewhat hardened by such an experience. Nothing would be further from the truth. Melitta Strandberg is a warm, caring and loving human being. It has been a pleasure and honor to work with her on this book.

George E Pfautsch

Introduction

"Hey kids, want some chocolates." Those words of American soldiers in 1945 would terminate a nightmarish journey to freedom for my parents, my siblings and me.

The end of our journey in 1945 marked the arrival of our refugee train in Augsburg, West Germany, which had earlier departed East Germany. On a track adjacent to our train was another train that had arrived at the same station and was fully loaded with American soldiers. They had arrived in Germany as World War II ended. The troops were there to protect and help rebuild the country that was to become my home.

When we arrived in Augsburg, I was only 8 months old and lying in a buggy. My parents parked the buggy under a light pole at the train station, and I was left there with my older sister and brother. At that time my sister was six years old and my brother was only four. We were left in my sister's care so my parents could procure our "arrival papers," which needed to be stamped and approved. My sister was holding on to my buggy with her small hands and also trying to watch my brother at the same time.

My brother, Willie, was intrigued with the nearby American soldiers, who were speaking in a strange and different language. However, at that moment the language of chocolate became universal. The soldiers were freely and eagerly handing out chocolates and chewing gum to us and the other refugee children that had just arrived. It was the first time that we had seen chocolate or any other candy.

One of the soldiers peeked into my buggy and said, "Hey little baby, I know you are too little for it, but when you get older, you can have some of this great American chocolate." Little did I know then, that 18 years later I would be eating plenty of those goodies.

Obviously, I don't recall these facts from my life at the age of 8 months, but this is my story as related to me by my mother and father.

Chapter 1

Life Before the Journey

My family's story began in Romania. Both of my parents were born in Romania during a troubled period of time. My father, Oskar Mohr, was born in Buhusi, Romania, on May 22, 1912, shortly before World War I, and my mother, Gisela Csek, was born in Buzau, Romania, on June 2, 1914, as World War I was about to begin.

World War I was a destructive war for Romania. Much of its army was captured or killed during the war and by May, 1918, it was in no position to continue the war and negotiated a peace treaty with Germany. It would re-enter the war later in the year. Following the war there was a significant addition and merging of countries in that region. Much of that was the result of the Treaty of Paris in 1920, and the region became known as Greater Romania.

Melitta Strandberg

The union of those numerous countries into Greater Romania resulted in the inclusion of various sizable minorities, which included ethnic Hungarians, Germans, Jews, Ukrainians, Bulgarians and several others. This was the Romania of my parents' youth.

The first and longest ruling government of Romania after World War I was a liberal constitutional monarchy. Due in large part to the expansion of minorities in Romania, especially Jews, the government faced the rise of nationalistic and anti-Semitic parties. The result was that King Carol II abolished the constitutional monarchy. Under King Carol II, Romania became a dictatorship.

My father attended a military academy in the region known as the "Sudetenland," a German region, within what is now Czechoslovakia. My father obtained his diploma (similar to a degree) in industrial engineering from the military academy in the Sudetenland, on September 24, 1931. He then returned to work

Oskar Mohr

in Romania. A few years later, in 1936, my parents were married. My father was of German heritage, whereas my mother was of Hungarian heritage. That seemingly insignificant difference in their background would play a troublesome role in later years. Sudetenland would become well known when Hitler would occupy it in the early stages of World War II. It was one of the earliest indications of his desire for world domination, but that lust of power would only become obvious to the world a few years later.

On February 3, 1939, their first child, my sister, Grete, was born. At that time, Romania was again in upheaval. Germany and the Soviet Union signed the Molotov-Ribbentrop Pact. As a result of the non-aggression pact between the two nations, they divided much of Eastern Europe into "spheres of influence." Romania fell under the Russian sphere of influence.

With a dictatorship ruling Romania and the Soviet Union being given much authority due to the Molotov-Ribbentrop Pact, life was becoming ever more turbulent and difficult for my parents and many other Romanians.

As World War II began, King Carol II tried to maintain Romania as a neutral country. But he was eventually forced into an agreement with Hitler. Through that process almost one-third of what was once Greater Romania became a part of other nations. Some lands were given to Russia, some to Hungary and some to Bulgaria.

Following these territorial losses, King Carol II was forced to abdicate and he was replaced by his son Mihai, but the real power was held by the military dictator, Ion Antonescu.

In 1941, my family was living in Buhusi, Romania, where my father was born. The country was in turmoil. Antonescu, a dictator of the worst kind, who would eventually be executed for war crimes, was making life unbearable for many people. He would eventually be found responsible for the death of more than 400,000 people, most of whom were Jews. Borders were not only being altered but sometimes closed.

That is one of the interesting and all too common stories of dictatorial rule. First they make life difficult for everyone and then they make sure no one escapes the miserable life they caused. Dictatorial rule occurs all too often in our world. In those situations, the inalienable right to freedom endowed by our Creator succumbs to those seeking more and more power, regardless of the price paid by the people.

The lack of freedom can be a terrible price for those who experience life without it. My mother and father experienced oppression too many years of their lives. This story has much to do with their personal quest for liberty.

Gisela Csek

My mother was also pregnant with a second child while my father was working as an engineer for a small textile factory in Buhusi. Life in Romania, under the Antonescu regime, was becoming ever more difficult.

This period of time was still three years prior to my birth. Therefore, I can only pass on to you some of the stories I recall my parents passing on to me.

I recall my parents telling me of one incident when they were living in Buhusi. One day some Russian soldiers came knocking at our door. I am not sure if my parents knew the reason, but I doubt that my father thought that it was going to be a friendly visit. He grabbed a large alarm clock and held it just inside the door. Dad told the Russians that he had a bomb and if they did not leave he would pull the wire connected to the bomb and everyone would be killed in the process. Being able to hear the ticking, they left rather hurriedly.

That type of incident does not make for peaceful and tranquil living. The rumors that communism might become a way of life was of deep concern to my parents. My father had a good job but Hitler was offering jobs in Germany and needed large numbers of people to fill them. Hitler was promising a better life in Germany which people wanted to hear.

Mother was in her final days of pregnancy with my brother, Willie. They made plans to settle in Germany. It would be a long trip that took some planning. By the time they had figured out the path they would take and also what items to pack or leave behind, my brother was born. In spite of the fact that they now had a tiny infant, it was time to leave.

Among other things, going to Germany meant a new language. My father was able to speak German, but my mother had to learn German from scratch. I recall her telling me that she learned German by reading her Bible.

Mother's prized possession was her sewing machine. She was a seamstress and that sewing machine simply was not going to be left behind. My father disassembled it and stored it under the mattress of the baby buggy that was carrying Willie. They were careful to store it in a manner that would not cause its detection. At that time the sewing machine was very important, as many of the family's clothes were made on it. Later on, other kids would envy us for being among the best-dressed. Mom took great pride in that.

It was a culmination of factors that convinced my parents to leave Romania. At some point in the life of human beings, situations, especially involving dictators, can become very stressful. Under such circumstances, people are often willing to forsake almost every material possession they have, (sewing machine excepted) in order to find freedom, especially when they also believe that they will find a better job situation. Unfortunately, when they left in 1941, they had no idea that they would be going from the frying pan into the fire.

Chapter 2

The First Phase of Our Journey

In late April of 1941, my father gathered the family together and goodbyes were said to our grandparents and other relatives. They would never see my grandparents again and it would be 29 very long years before they would see any of their other relatives. My parents were not even able to return for the funerals of my grandparents.

Almost all of our possessions had to be left behind when my family departed by train during the night. Their journey that evening began in Buhusi, Romania, and would slowly transport them to Weimar, Germany.

It was not necessarily a dangerous trip but there were some risk-filled experiences in many ways. There were numerous stops along the way and what few possessions they had would be checked. But the sewing machine was never discovered. That was a big relief to my parents, especially my mother. Had the sewing machine been discovered it could have been confiscated and my parents could have been ordered back to Romania or even jailed.

The journey lasted several days. With everything else to worry about, my mother's experience was almost beyond our imaginative capabilities. The unknown situation that was awaiting them, a new language to learn, very few possessions, and the birth of a new child are memories that will always be a reminder of the courageousness of my mother. She was, is and will always be my heroine. She was yet to endure much more.

My father too was a courageous man. Over the next four years, he would find himself in dangerous situations and would have to use many ingenious tactics to protect us and himself.

Following the family's arrival in Weimar, Germany, it did not take long for my father to find employment. Not long after our arrival in Weimar my father became the Chief Engineer at the "Gusslovwerke," a German ammunition factory. Life seemed to be on track again. Initially, that was true.

The immediate situation in Weimar was an improvement of my family's life compared with Romania. But even as they arrived there, events taking place in Germany were rapidly changing life for German people and those who had immigrated there.

Even though Germany was waging war in 1941, it was still a land of promise for many. The German economy grew by leaps and bounds under Hitler. He had built the Volkswagen, autobahns, and numerous factories. Compared with the long Depression following World War I, the German people were prospering under Hitler during the 1930's and even into the early 1940's.

During the early part of his regime, his brutal tactics were not that obvious. After that long Depression that followed World War I, the German people had some legitimate reasons to initially like his regime. No other country was more prosperous and people were flocking to Germany to find employment. My parents were among those people.

In 1941, the dark clouds of war were becoming more apparent and more widespread, but it was still early in the war and the Nazis were having success in the military aspects of the war, even though unjustified success. Also in 1941, Hitler had already brought Austria into the German Republic, and occupied the Sudetenland of Czechoslovakia, which as noted earlier, was home to many German settlers who were happy to be reunited with the homeland.

Those of you, who have seen the "Sound of Music," have some idea of what was happening in Austria in the late 1930's. The Von Trapp family, featured in that film, had to make some of the same type decisions my family also made.

By 1941, Hitler's armies had also invaded Poland and France. Along with the Italians, they also occupied territories of North Africa. London was being bombed. In many ways, Hitler was truly "having success" on the battlefield. As one can imagine, the factories were also busy putting out the machines of war.

In June of 1941, Hitler's army also invaded Russia. Then in December of 1941, following the attack on Pearl Harbor by the Japanese, the United States was brought into the war. Hitler was now fighting wars on many fronts and the war would soon turn against him. As the war began turning against the Nazis, the lives of people living within Germany would become a living hell.

Chapter 3

Life in Weimar, Germany

I am not exactly sure how much knowledge my parents had of the aforementioned military events, but not too long after they arrived in Weimar, their lives would again take a bleak turn, along with all others living in Germany.

Many of these military events were occurring at about the time my family arrived in Weimar. One event that would prove to be disastrous for them was Hitler's attack on Russia in mid-1941. The effects of this were not immediate for us, but when the counter-attack from the Russians came, it would have a great impact on our lives in 1945.

It started becoming more obvious to more people that Hitler's plans went beyond his lust of dominating the nations of Europe and possibly the world.

It became known that Hitler was intent on creating a "master race." He was also intent on destroying and eliminating the Jewish race. The building of his "master race" also put foreigners within Germany at risk. My family was at risk. As noted earlier, although my parents were both born in Romania, my father was of German heritage and my mother was of Hungarian heritage.

Just five miles from the city of Weimar, was the infamous Buchenwald prison camp. My parents' home was near Buchenwald on the outskirts of Weimar towards the area of that terrible camp. They would witness the thousands of people who were in long lines and loaded on to and off of trucks and trains, never to be seen again. These people had to wear bands on their arms with blue stars painted on them.

Buchenwald was one of the worst of the Nazi prisons. It is estimated that almost a quarter of a million prisoners were held there at some time and that more than 56,000 people died there.

Once again, it is painful to think about the experience of my parents and siblings. There were rumors about the atrocities. At times, my parents would take walks near Buchenwald and would hear the gunfire, and could see some of the mass graves. I believe they understood something about the Jews who were there and who were permitted to starve and die. The cries could be heard at night if you were within a quarter mile of the camp.

Life during 1942 and 1943 became increasingly worse for my family. The war became more intense and cities in the region were now being bombed more frequently by the Allied forces. The cities became piles of rubble.

As the war continued my father was drafted as a medic in the spring of 1944. My mother would again go through another extremely difficult period. Her husband was gone and she was left alone to care for my sister and brother.

While she was at home alone with my brother and sister, I can only imagine how difficult it was for her. She would often have to wait in line to try to get what little food might be available. Everything was rationed. My brother and sister would sometimes have to go to bed hungry. Mom would tell us how painful it was to experience that. In addition to standing in lines she would go through garbage cans to find food. She also would sometimes create a meal out of potato peelings. That kind of living is hard for us to imagine. In addition to those hardships she was again pregnant.

Chapter 4

Sept 3, 1944 And Subsequent Events

On September 3rd, 1944, I was born in a hospital in Weimar. My parents were unaware that this particular hospital also served as Hitler's operation for selecting newborn and young children for experimental purposes. That was especially true for babies born to parents from Poland, Romania, Hungary and Yugoslavia. Once again the foreign nationality of my mother may have played a role.

We were not a part of Hitler's "pure race," which he intended for Germany. Shortly after my birth, I was taken from my mother and vanished.

I was later told that a different baby was given to mom hours later for feeding. My mother refused and told them she was not going to accept this baby because it was not hers. They took that baby away but I was not returned to her.

My mother had one recollection of my birth in the few minutes I was with her. She remembered that I had a birthmark on my lower arm. That birthmark would become a significant identification at a later period.

One can only imagine the trauma my parents felt and their frantic search to locate me. They looked many places and many doors were shut in their faces. Lies were told to them, including that I had died. Regardless of what they were told my parents remained determined to find me and to also find answers and the truth.

Both Mom and Dad were in a state of mourning, but they continued to look and search everywhere possible. They would pass out notes to others in hopes that someone might know something.

My father heard that Hitler had a secret medical facility in the neighboring town of Jena. Rumors also had it that this institute was being used for experimentation on the captured children and babies. It later became known that reproductive systems were being removed from the older children and often younger children were "guinea pigs" for the development of drugs. Some large pharmaceutical companies were complicit in these experiments.

Among some of the experiments were those to produce Hitler's "master race." Based on their inquiries, my parents suspected that I had been taken there for experimental purposes. However, they were not certain nor were they sure where the Jena Institute was located.

In the world today, we decry that such human experimentation could have taken place. But too often we still continue to devalue human life in many places, including our own country.

And to add to our misery, Dad, a regular soldier in the German army for a brief time, was captured by American Forces a few months later. They had approximately 200 prison camps around Germany. Luckily Dad's imprisonment lasted only a few weeks. After he was let go, he found his way home, shed his uniform and never returned to the military. We were a family again.

Dad looked back and said things could have been worse. Many German soldiers were taken to Siberia and never returned. Those prisoners were marched to the Russian front. The cold and wet spring had gotten the best of them. The lack of clothing on their backs, and good shoes, pushed them to the limit. Many of them were found lying face-down in the mud -- starvation, and disease overcame them. And to ensure that they would be quickly forgotten and never again identified, their dog-tags were cut in half, their bodies were covered with chemicals for rapid decomposition and buried. How lucky Dad was to have been taken prisoner by American troops. The treatment by far was so much better.

You can imagine the happy reunion to once again be a whole family. Praise be to God.

Mom and Dad, once reunited, resumed the search for me. By now, six long painful months elapsed and their knowledge of my whereabouts remained a mystery.

By this time, my parents, sister and brother were living in a single room in a camp where people were being housed who wished to migrate to the west. Not only were they cramped in a room that was about 12 by 17 feet, but it was shared with another family. The word "cramped" is no doubt a gross understatement.

One evening, about six months after I vanished, my family and the other family were huddled in their cramped quarters. It was a particularly bitter cold evening. A freezing wind and snow were part of that night. My mother heard some noise outside of our quarters. There was no heat in the room and they did not want to open the door because it would let more cold air inside.

Mother scraped the ice off the window to find out what was happening. She saw someone running away from the building, so she quickly opened the door to inquire, but the person kept on running.

At that point, my mother looked down at the doorstep and there was a large cardboard box, which appeared to be filled with rags. She then heard a faint cry from the box. She pulled in the box, and rummaged through the rags. There was a tiny baby, with its arm reaching out and the birthmark she did not forget. She knew immediately that it was me. Despite the cold, and despite the terrible facilities in which they lived, there was great joy in that cramped little room that evening.

Although my parents did not give up their search for me, after six months they never really expected to see me alive again.

When I was reunited with my family, I was very

much undernourished and unable to function as a six month old baby. It was a challenge to return me to normal health. I had also contracted jaundice of some sort.

As noted earlier, on the evening I was returned, the person that brought me to the camp where my family was residing ran away and therefore no questions of what had happened to me were answered at that time.

My parents did discover later that I was in fact taken to a place where hundreds of children were kept and subjected to experimentation. Nevertheless, the things that may have happened to me there remain a mystery and will undoubtedly remain a mystery. It is something I still think about, but it is also something I have learned to deal with.

Hitler's experimental hospitals were discovered but it was simply too late for some. Many children, who had been displaced during the war, could not be returned to their parents. Those children were placed in orphanages. Many starved to death. Others simply disappeared.

Reuniting me with my parents was indeed God's miracle. It will always be thought of by me in that way.

The Lord's wishes were that somehow I would be one of the very few, who miraculously was selected to be taken to the holding camp, and brought back to my mother's arms. There are no coincidences with God. I am a believer of that.

I know that I have mentioned it earlier, but once again I must mention that my mother is my heroine. My entire family is special in ways others cannot possibly understand. My Savior is special in ways that may be difficult for others to understand. He gave me the chance to live a life on this earth far longer than seemed possible for those who wondered about my whereabouts during that cold winter of 1944/45. A meager holding camp room of 12 by 17 feet can be a beautiful home.

Chapter 5

The Last Year in Weimar

In addition to my disappearance, other things that occurred during the last year my family lived in Weimar, which was from mid-1944 to mid-1945, caused life for us to become an even worse living inferno. The war for the Germans was slowly but surely being lost. People were being killed and displaced. Buchenwald was a nightmare. Other geopolitical and military situations would add to the pain of my family.

During the last year of our lives in Weimar, the war became more intense. The city of Weimar was unrecognizable. What was once a city of great culture, famous art galleries and precious architectural palaces, was now a pile of rubble.

I obviously cannot recall the events of that period of time and therefore I can again only repeat the stories my family told me of that final, terrible year in Weimar. Hopefully these stories will provide some faint idea of what life was like at that time for my family.

One day my father had to take my mom to a dentist and on their way there they had to cross some railroad tracks. The Americans had targeted the railroads for bombing to stop the transportation of troops and armaments.

On this particular day a bombing raid occurred just as my parents were crossing the tracks. They had no time to find a shelter. They dove to the ground immediately in a fairly open area, which my dad quickly realized was not a good place for them. He grabbed mom and quickly moved to a different place he believed would be safer. As soon as they reached the safer place, bombs fell on the exact spot from which they had moved. Both were covered with dirt but alive and unharmed. Without that quick decision to move from their initial position, my siblings and I would have been orphans.

On another occasion, when my parents were out looking for food, my older sister, brother and I had to be left home alone. At that point my sister was six years old, my brother four and I was an infant. As the bomb sirens started, my sister grabbed my brother, put me into a large pillowcase and ran out to the street to try to find the nearest bunker. The noise of the sirens was so loud that we could not hear the planes swooping down toward us and laying down a trail of bullets behind us. Still running, a stranger ran out of his house, grabbed the three of us and got us safely into the bunker. My sister certainly got a crash course in survival, not in Girls Scout, but in the bomb shelter. If that nice man had not helped us, my parents would have instantly become childless.

The winter lingered on longer than usual that last year in Weimar. There was no food and no heat. It sometimes became necessary to search for food scraps in garbage cans. Food lines were very long and my mom often stood in lines for hours for small amounts of bread, milk or potatoes. There was never enough food for all of us, but my mother's creative cooking skills went a long way. She was not only a great cook, but as previously noted, also a great seamstress.

That sewing machine my parents had smuggled out of Romania would prove very valuable. She would find scrap clothing and manage to somehow sew some clothing together for us.

I recall my sister telling me that when our shoes became too small for our growing feet, Dad would cut out the leather area by the front tip of our shoes so our toes would have enough room to grow. That way they did not have to get us new shoes. I have had foot problems my entire life.

In April, 1945, Patton's Third Army would move into Weimar and occupy the city. Unfortunately for my family, President Roosevelt and the other Allied leaders had promised at the Yalta Conference to put Eastern Germany, including Weimar, under Soviet Union rule.

It became known that the Russians were planning to seal the border between East and West Germany. Almost too late, my parents discovered that there was going to be a final train leaving for West Germany.

Once more my parents had to make a hasty decision to get out and go west, and this time it was out of Weimar, which was soon to be occupied by the Soviet Union. A hurried decision was again made to take the risk to seek freedom.

Chapter 6

The Journey to the West

The new border between East and West Germany had been part of the Yalta Agreement. The Russians were taking steps to seal off that border so emigration could be stopped.

My parents discovered on short notice that the last transport train was about to leave and if we were not on it, we would be destined to remain in the hell hole, that Weimar had become for us. My father, constantly faced the threat of being taken to Siberia, and stranding my mother in a terrible place, under terrible conditions, with her three small children.

Mom and Dad made the quick decision to try to catch that last train. By now they had become somewhat experts in ways to escape under difficult circumstances. Some of that expertise was about to become more apparent. With little more than the clothes on our backs, the decision was made to leave. The border was about to be sealed.

But some things had to happen first. One was that our papers had to be in order and two was that we had to be screened for health purposes. We had to move in a hurry. It literally was going to be the last train out of East Germany.

The first thing that needed to be done was to get our papers in order, the most important being transfer papers. As we approached the area to obtain our documents, we encountered a very long line of other people trying to do the same thing.

The time had come for my father's creative escape expertise. As we stood in the back of the line, my father moved to the side of the line and began moving forward. He began impersonating an official and as he moved forward he pretended to count each and every person in the line. It worked and very shortly he found himself at the head of the line. I truly believe that this idea was inspired by God. How else could we have made it in time?

Then came step two. When he reached the person with "real" authority, my father produced a piece of paper from his pocket and handed it to the person in charge. On that piece of paper, my father had written our address, and noted that if the person in charge would go there he would find some furniture, coal, potatoes and other food items. At that time people would do almost anything for food and materials to heat their home. The man in charge was no exception.

In a very short period of time we had obtained our papers. We were permitted one piece of luggage, the kids were to be carried on my parents' backs and, oh yes, I was in the baby buggy. It too would serve a good purpose other than just transporting me.

Very shortly, after securing the necessary papers, we boarded the last transport train to freedom or whatever one might wish to call that train. It was more like a cattle car. It does deserve a little more description.

A stinky locomotive pulled about 15 boxcars with no windows, toilets or seats. The inside of the boxcars contained bales of hay on which people could sit. It was quickly apparent that people also urinated on those bales of hay. The stench was almost unbearable, but with the price of freedom sometimes comes the smell of urination, defecation, body odors and a few other odors. People were pushed in like cattle, which they probably once transported in that boxcar. It was standing room only, but there was no entertainment. Nevertheless, to my parents, simply making that train, made it seem like a trip to some resort location.

That trip however was going to have some flashbacks to the tyranny we were leaving. The trip to the western border had many twists and checkpoints. The train would stop at times accompanied by lots of yelling from outside the train. Women would cry while men were removed from the train and taken away from their families.

My mom, dad, Grete, Willie and I were crowded into a corner of the boxcar. They later told me that I was very sick on the trip. I had a severe case of jaundice, as previously noted, which either lingered or reappeared and which put me in an almost comatose type sleep. That was actually some good news along with the bad news. The sleep kept me from crying and drawing attention to us. The bad news was that there was again doubt if I would be alive when we reached the west. We had our fears but also faith in God to pull us through these difficult steps of this part of the journey.

My parents were hoping that we would reach the border in a matter of hours, but that was not to be the case. My parents would often later say that if they were uncertain about what hell was like, they found out on that train. There were no windows - there was no light - there was no food and for sure there was no fresh air. If the stench from everything else was not bad enough, the stench from vomit was added as many people were sick or suffered motion sickness by the winding motion of the train. Where was the Environmental Protection Agency when we needed them? I guess sometimes the search for freedom is enough to keep one alive.

After moving for some hours, the train suddenly came to a stop. There was mud all around the tracks. After sitting like ducks on a hunting pond and not having any idea what was happening, my father proceeded to step out of the boxcar along with a few other people to ascertain the reason for the stop. They quickly discovered that the locomotive had been uncoupled from the boxcars. Freedom was delayed once more.

My father and the others walked to a house near the end of the tracks. The boxcars were now on a dead end side track and there was no locomotive in sight. The people in the house were uniformed. My father and others were told that the train was still in the east sector of Germany and they were preparing to "de-lice" everyone on board. That also meant that papers would again be checked and the necessary stamp had to be displayed or else the ride to the west was over.

My dad, ever fearful of being sent to Siberia, suspected this was another trap to select engineers who the Russians needed. This time my dad's concerns proved very legitimate. One officer, who was friendly to my father, informed him not to enter through a certain door at the checkpoint, because it was therein that they were checking and scanning papers looking for engineers. Obviously, Dad followed his advice and had our papers checked at a different point. Things went fine and after a few hours we could feel the train moving, and we were again heading to the west sector. Why the delay? The old locomotive had to stay in the east sector, while a locomotive from the west sector was hooked up to our boxcars.

Those Russians just could not do enough checking. After a few hours we again stopped and the door opened on our boxcar. A Russian soldier wearing his official badge was obviously going to check papers one more time. But before he did that, he first begged those on the train for cigarettes. My parents wondered why in the world he was asking that of the poor refugees on the train. As soon as he asked for the cigarettes another

Russian soldier, who must have been his superior, came up to the soldier and began reprimanding him.

My father understood Russian, and later told us roughly what the senior soldier said, "Hey you stupid bastard, you want them to poison you?" After a few minutes the door on our boxcar was suddenly closed. There was no checking of papers. Why? Well, my father later found out that our boxcar and the one adjoining us were painted the same color. In the confusion with the cigarettes, the soldier mistakenly checked the adjoining car twice and assumed on the second check that he was checking ours. At that time, we were just thankful for such mishaps. Later in life, my parents could look on that incident with some humor.

There is one more situation related to the trip out of Weimar that I must share with you. As you recall, the only things we could take were the clothes we were wearing and one piece of luggage, and, oh yes, that baby carriage that held me. That little buggy not only carried me but also my mother's prized possession. It was the sewing machine which she also had brought from Romania, and which she used so adeptly to make our clothes.

My father had disassembled it once more and

stored it below me in the baby buggy in which I was lying, much as was done when they stored it under Willie's mattress on the journey out of Romania. Some things were just too precious to be left behind. In their never-ending checks, it could easily have been discovered. Why was it not discovered? Each time we were stopped, my parents told those checking that I was very ill and could not possibly be disturbed. That to a large degree was true.

In any event, they never did disturb me or that sewing machine. During the war, a sewing machine really was a prized asset. Mom arrived at her destination with her prized asset along with a somewhat comatose child. The state I was in, as noted earlier, did have the one and only positive effect of keeping me quiet on the trip.

Our journey from Weimar would take two entire days on that broken down train. That trip today could be made in a few hours by car.

After so very many stops, the train finally pulled into that beautiful town of Augsburg, Germany, which was to become our home in the West. As we pulled into the station, we saw electric street lights for the first time. We found Augsburg and finally, finally, finally we had freedom.

Chapter 7

Freedom

"Hey kids, want some chocolates." Somehow those words, later told to me by my parents and sister, have had special memories for me all of my life. To me they are associated with freedom. That may sound a little strange, but it is nevertheless true. Our arrival in Augsburg, Germany, would indeed end the many years my parents searched for freedom.

For so many of us freedom has always been a way of life and we take it for granted. My parents never took it for granted and neither do I. The founding fathers of this nation had it right. People on this earth, are endowed by their Creator with the inalienable rights of life and liberty. It is despots and tyrants, who take away those rights. They should never be taken for granted and all of us need to be vigilant to ensure that those precious rights are never lost.

This story you are reading has been on my mind for many years and I have taken many steps at writing it, but never really had the feeling that it was in the form to be put into a book.

Not too long ago, a friend of mine told me of a childhood acquaintance who was now an author. After contacting him several times he read the rough manuscript I had prepared. After digging into the story, he agreed to provide help and he also agreed to co-author this book with me. Initially, this story as written by me ended with our arrival in Augsburg.

He believed and convinced me that there was more to the story and that the rest of my life would also be interesting to readers. He believed people would want to know what happened to that little baby in the buggy. He also believed that the book begged for thoughts about the meaning of freedom to us, who had been deprived of it in early life and whose parents were deprived of it for many years.

My co-author has written a number of books which express his fondness for our founding fathers and the great love they had for their faith and for freedom. He knows that the day, July 4th, is very important to me because of its significance to freedom. That date also has a second special significance to me for another reason, which will become apparent later.

Since it was such a special day in my life, he thought it would be a nice symbolic touch to begin the draft of this chapter on July 4th, 2010, the 234th birthday of our country. That was the date this chapter began.

It is also the date that my pastor and I did a joint presentation at our church on the Manhattan Declaration. That declaration is intended to promote, among other things, the importance of religious liberty to our nation and to the people of all nations.

Our arrival, in Augsburg, transformed life for my entire family. Until arriving in Augsburg, freedom was only a dream. In Romania and again in Weimar we simply did not understand what it meant to be free. We lived in the constant fear of what might happen to us as a family and as individuals. One's life was subjected to the whims of government. Those types of governments ignore the words of our third president, Thomas Jefferson. "The care of human life and happiness, and not their destruction, is the first and only legitimate objective of good government."

Freedom of speech and freedom of religion were non-existent for my family in the years prior to 1945.

Uttering the wrong words at the wrong time could quickly make you an enemy of the state. Going to a church to worship was out of the question.

Being a foreigner also meant discrimination. While the Jewish people suffered the greatest atrocities, other nationalities in Weimar were also selected for discrimination. The German citizens themselves had to be on guard, lest they offended the Nazi regime.

Justice was meted out as befit the whims of the Nazis and especially the dreaded SS troopers. One's freedom could be terminated for no apparent reason.

The war that raged in Germany, especially during the latter years, also denied many the ability to obtain shelter or food. Life was a daily struggle for self-subsistence.

I often wonder how my parents had the courage to undertake the many risks they took to escape tyranny. While the magnet of freedom was no doubt a part of it, I suspect they often believed life simply was not worth living under the circumstances they were experiencing.

In this nation, we believe God endowed us with the inalienable right to life, but to those living in tyrannical situations, that right seems very elusive.

It has often been said that one of the prices we must pay for freedom is vigilance. Life and freedom are inalienable rights, but those rights are not automatic in this world. Millions of brave people have died to defend and protect those rights. This nation has had a proud history of defending those rights, not only for its own citizens, but for the rights of citizens of other countries.

I not only have a love of those who gave us chocolates, because they gave the chocolates, but also because they were on the front lines of protecting freedom.

Sometimes the citizens of this nation take freedom for granted. Apathy is a great risk to the preservation of freedom. Governments must sometimes be reminded of the words of our second President, John Adams, "You have rights antecedent to all earthly governments; rights that cannot be repealed or restrained by human laws; rights derived from the Great Legislator of the universe." When any government forgets those words it also forgets the reason for governments to exist.

My family discovered those rights. For my parents it was a long, long struggle to find the government that remembered those words of our second president. For their endless search to find freedom, they will always have my deepest love and my deepest respect.

While writing this chapter, my co-author asked me if there were any comments I would give to fellow Americans regarding freedom.

My response follows:

> *Never, never take freedom for granted. It is an inalienable right granted to us by God, but there have been too many evil doers throughout history, who have controlled governments who would take that precious gift of God from us. Citizens must be vigilant.*
>
> *Several years ago, my husband and I decided we would take a long trip along the east coast to learn more about the history of our nation. Our trip would last 85 days. It started in Maine and took us to Florida. Our stops included Boston, Philadelphia, Washington, D.C., including the Capitol and the White House, Williamsburg and many other historical cities. We learned about the founding fathers along with other people and events that led to our Declaration of Independence, and our great Constitution including the Bill of Rights. We became familiar with their struggles to achieve freedom, including religious freedom. I would urge all citizens of this nation to understand those sacrifices so all would have a greater appreciation of freedom.*
>
> *"The God who gave us life gave us liberty at*

the same time," said Thomas Jefferson. We must now preserve our liberty with our involvement in such things as the Manhattan Declaration and other actions. We must vote for those who share the love of freedom and not be afraid to voice our opinions and concerns to our elected officials.

I have come to deeply love this country and what it stands for, but much has changed and is changing. We must be vigilant against those who wittingly or unwittingly destroy our freedom. Bad politicians can do that.

Please be willing to stand up and fight for that freedom even as those who died on the battlefield have been willing to do and as our forefathers did. This is a country comprised of us who were legal immigrants or had parents, grandparents, etc. who found a home here because this nation allowed us and still allows us to live in peace and prosperity.

Chapter 8

Life in Augsburg

As I noted earlier, we had to leave Weimar with very few possessions. That really was not a big problem for us. We did not have many possessions in Weimar. When we arrived in Augsburg, Germany we had the clothes we were wearing, a few things in the one piece of luggage we were permitted to carry along, my baby buggy and, oh yes, mom's sewing machine.

That did not matter. We had each other and we were free. There were no more bombings. There were no more trains into and out of Buchenwald. There were no more Russian soldiers checking everything. Very simply, we no longer had to live in fear. We had what every government owes its people; the inalienable right to freedom.

Life finally took on a normal pace. Just as the tree

comes to life in spring, our family came alive as the blossoms come alive.

Although Augsburg was very heavily damaged from the war, reconstruction was already on its way. Beautiful glass stained windows that were taken to basements during the war, so not to suffer the damage from bombardments, were recovered and placed back into the cathedrals. I am proud to say that today they look untouched. Some of them are 800 years old. Rather than level historic buildings that were so damaged, reconstructions took place, and the city once more stood proud by the mid 50's.

Soon after arriving in Augsburg, my father found employment with the maker of electric appliances, AEG, as an electrical engineer.

My dad was a wonderful father, husband and provider to his family. You have read of the many risks he had to take to get his family to Augsburg. I would also like to tell you more of his professional and personal life.

In the 1950's my father became the Chief Engineer for a large textile plant "Prince A. G." in Augsburg. He was one of their top employees. Other companies, such as Siemens A. G. often sought him out to solve problems which they encountered. At Christmas time, my family would receive baskets of goodies from many of the companies he helped. He was truly a talented and well-liked man. We were very proud of him.

He was not only a top-notch engineer where he was employed, but he enjoyed doing scientific projects as a hobby. He often gave lectures on these projects at universities in the Augsburg and Munich region.

Dad also had a large collection of preserved butterflies. This hobby kept him busy many evenings. After his death, my mother donated his collection to an exhibit hall in Munich, Germany. An associated hobby was taxidermy. In my hallway, I still have a cute little squirrel perched on a branch, which is a product of my father's hobby.

My father was also a violinist. We all listened in awe when he brought it out to play for family and friends. He was also an excellent gymnast. He could swing on those parallel bars with the best. Given the difficult life he experienced, I often have marveled that he somehow found the time to learn these hobbies and skills.

Despite the difficulties he experienced in life he had a great sense of humor. He and my sister would often dress in funny clothing in the evenings and do humorous impersonations that would keep the rest of us in stitches.

Sadly my dad passed away at an early age. I am sure that experiences of World War II together with the chemical fumes from the textile factory took their toll. During the war he also became a smoker and never kicked that habit. Sometimes there was nothing to eat, but somehow cigarettes could be found.

My older sister, Grete, began elementary school and she was soon followed by my brother, Willie, and me. It was a tradition, that when children began school in Augsburg, they would be given a large cone filled with fruits and candies. It is a wonderful tradition.

As was true of so many cities in Germany during World War II, Augsburg also suffered damage. There were many things that needed rebuilding and many landmarks that were being renovated. Many buildings had the swastika engraved or painted above the entrance. Removing that symbol was a high priority.

I hate to admit that my own birth certificate still bears the swastika symbol. I have carried that hated Nazi symbol with me my entire life. At this point, maybe some white-out would not upset authorities in this country.

Upon arrival in Augsburg, my parents initially lived in a small apartment. Some of the rubble gave my dad an idea. First he bought a small piece of land in the countryside. Then he decided he could do two good deeds; one for our family and the other to aid in the clean-up of the city. He would save money on buying bricks and also help clean up the rubble by gathering the bricks that were once part of buildings.

This then is how we spent many weekends. My dad had a large wooden wagon. On weekends he would load my sister, my brother and me into that wagon and pull us into town. That exercise included pulling that wagon more than five miles each trip. My dad would gather and clean at least 100 of those bricks each trip, load them into the wagon and take them to the land he bought. With those bricks came the first major capital investment of our family; a house of our own. Dad hauled those bricks many weekends and then would slowly build our first home.

I remember an interesting little story connected with the building of that house. On June 20, 1948, West Germany abolished the Reich Mark currency and converted to a new Deutsche Mark. That created a short-term currency shortage. I remember Dad saying that he was the only one who had enough money the next day to buy a wash basin for the house. He was very proud and said as he entered the house, "Nobody will be dirty in this house." Mom was thrilled as she could also use it to wash her dishes. After years of being deprived of many things, it was amazing how many uses one could find for that little sink.

The house, by standards of today, was nothing fancy, but it was special to us. It was our home in a free land. It was not far from the city and I recall that it overlooked potato fields. We would love to watch the farmer come by with his tractor and plow the fields. When the farmer was in a good mood, he would tell one of us watching him to hop on his tractor. That was a great treat. We pretended that we were riding in a car sitting up high and showing off. In fact, the tractor was slower than a horse.

Once my father completed the house, my parents would invite many friends to our home, who had also escaped from the eastern-bloc countries. There were many of them in the Augsburg area. They would share stories of their lives prior to arriving in the western zone. The kids were not allowed to listen, although we would hold a glass to the other side of the wall of the room in which they were talking so we could eavesdrop in on those stories.

Hey Kids, Want Some Chocolates?

Our parents always intended to tell us the story of their experiences someday, but not while we were so young, in fear that it would traumatize us. My mother never told me "my story" until I was 16 years old. At that time she told me a great deal of "my story." It took me 45 years and a lot of encouragement from my husband, Herb, to write my story.

As a youth, I experienced some health problems with my lungs. There were frequent trips for me to the mountains which seemed to help me recuperate. We never completely understood the problem. If it was associated with the events of the first year of my life, I will probably never know. But today there are no symptoms of those problems. Again, I am thankful to my mother for the wonderful care she gave me, even under the worst of conditions.

School was a great experience. The exception to that was my English teacher. She would punish students rather severely if they did not

Melitta Strandberg at 6

pronounce English words exactly as she pronounced them. In those days spankings were permitted and she did it in the front of the room for everyone to see. If my recollections are correct, I was frequently the "guest of honor" in the front of that class.

One subject I particularly enjoyed in elementary school was art and I was quite good at it. Art was a mandatory subject in German schools at that time. That class and my love of art would stand me in good stead in future years. Sometimes I would help my fellow classmates with their art and they would help me with my math. That aptitude for art has been rewarding. Today, I frequently work in my art studio drawing and painting floral designs on silk scarves.

We had a long walk to and from school each day. It was especially difficult and tiresome when there was lots of snow. Augsburg is not that far from the German Alps and snow could sometimes accumulate up to four feet in some areas.

Our favorite pastime was playing with the neighborhood kids. My family also raised rabbits, but that was good news and bad news. The good news is that I would get attached to my little furry friends. The bad news is that those rabbits were not being raised with

Hey Kids, Want Some Chocolates?

the intent to become our pets. Rather they became rabbit stew. I remember one occasion when I was particularly attached to one of those cute little rabbits. I was afraid he too was soon to become rabbit stew, so one evening I crawled into the cage and slept all night with the rabbit. I was hoping that somehow that would persuade my dad to spare him. Even that did not work. I finally realized that none of those little bunnies were ever going to stay around long enough to be a pet.

In addition to sewing, (oh yes, she still had the sewing machine) my mother also loved gardening. Most of the vegetables we ate were grown by her. We also grew fruit trees. One problem our parents had with that was that we kids would crawl up those trees and eat some plums before they had a chance to ripen. I do not recall if Imodium was around at that time.

Melitta, Willie & Grete

Although I have mentioned mother's skills as a seamstress, mom spent most of her life as a homemaker and she was very good at it. She did love to sew and made us many clothes from the excess material my father would bring home from the textile factory. She would design our garments and my sister and I wore those proudly. We received many compliments on our clothes, thanks to her efforts.

Mom also loved cooking, baking and, as noted earlier, gardening. She taught me many of her skills and often told me that if you want to make a man happy, learn to be a neat housekeeper and a good cook. I have tried to follow that advice.

It was a true delight to have mom spend her days at home. Dinner would always be ready for us when we arrived home from school or work.

Melitta, mother & Grete

Hey Kids, Want Some Chocolates?

Our home was a musical home. As I have already mentioned, Dad was a violinist. My sister played the flute and I played the piano. Everyone else would join in singing songs and hymns to praise the Lord. After our early years, we had many reasons to praise the Lord.

After we had been in Augsburg for a few years, our parents gave us a surprise. Ten years after I was born my mother gave birth to our brother, Alexander. It was a delight to have a baby in the house and we all took turns spoiling him.

Little brother Alexander

I graduated from elementary school in the late 1950's and went on to higher education. Following school I took a civil service exam and obtained a good job in the government's social security office. I worked as an apprentice in the social security data center. That too would prove useful in later life. Getting accepted for that position was one of the highlights of my life. I thank the Lord frequently for giving me the knowledge to pass that difficult test with a good score. It is truly

God that provides us humans with our talents and for that I have been very grateful.

    As I approached my late teen years, there would be new and different directions to my life.

Chapter 9

July 4, 1963

During my teenage years, there were events happening in my life that would frequently make me think of life in the United States. It was not that life in Augsburg was not rewarding compared with the lives my parents had lived. But, as is true of many teenagers, wanderlust and the thought of greener pastures would frequently enter my mind.

My older sister had met a wonderful American soldier name Richard. She had met him through our German-American church gatherings. Our family thought highly of Richard but his tour of duty would soon end. Before that happened Grete and Richard became engaged. Six months later, he would return to Germany and they were married. They would return to the United States and live near Minneapolis. I was still not old enough to date, but their marriage alone triggered thoughts of moving to this country.

I had also gotten to know other American military men and their wives. They all seemed to be very much at ease and their demeanor always seemed to be very friendly. In my early teenage years, I sometimes baby sat for the young children of American military families. My English was still very poor (just elementary school level) but that universal language of food hit me again.

Just as my brother Willie became intrigued with the chocolates that the American troops had given him, so I became with that new delicacy called, "ice cream." I did not babysit for money. That ice cream was pay enough. Ice cream as wonderful and flavorful as that which could be bought at the American Exchange did not hit the German grocery shelves until the early 1970's.

One day, when I was 16, my mom and dad took me to a Billy Graham crusade in Stuttgart, Germany. Everything was translated from English to German for us. That night I made the decision that Christ would be a part of my life. A few weeks later I was baptized at our German Baptist church.

Time wise, that crusade was concurrent with my decision to go to the United States. I proceeded to ask

Hey Kids, Want Some Chocolates?

my parents' permission to immigrate to this country. Initially, they would not allow it and said I was simply too young and immature for that to happen.

At that time my sister and brother-in-law were still living near Minneapolis. They assured my parents that if I came to live in their area, they would keep an eye on me.

When I was about to turn 17, my parents finally permitted me to apply for all the necessary immigration papers, and after eleven months the US consulate finally stamped the seal of approval on all the necessary documents.

Alex, dad and mom seeing me depart for the USA

During those years of waiting, I would often look at the sun setting in the west and blow it a kiss as it disappeared. I would also imagine as it set over Augsburg, that it was shining brightly over the United States and that one day I would follow it there.

Finally, the day of departure arrived. I bid my parents and family farewell. They knew and trusted that I was going to a God-loving country. After all even the money states "In God We Trust."

I arrived in the United States on July 4th, 1963 during the evening hours. I saw the display of fireworks all around the city of Minneapolis as we were landing. I thought all those fireworks were for my arrival. My thoughts at that time were about the same as that famous comedian, Yakov Smirnoff, who often states, "WHAT A COUNTRY!!!" I was just sure my sister had told people I was coming and I thought "Praise the Lord, what a reception."

Then I discovered that freedom was celebrated in the United States in this manner every year. My ego was somewhat put back in place, but I enjoyed my entrance to this country very much. Now life in this precious new country of mine was to begin.

Chapter 10

A Life of Freedom and Faith in God

When I arrived in the United States, I lived with my sister, Grete, and her husband, Richard. For a period of time they provided me room and board, which was much appreciated by me. Their home was in Northfield, Minnesota, not too far south of the Minneapolis/St. Paul area.

I began familiarizing myself with the area and soon went to work for G.T. Sheldahl, Inc., which manufactured atmospheric research balloons. Language was still a barrier for me, but I learned quickly. While there, I made many new friends with whom I am still in touch.

I married James Jacobson in 1964 who was also employed with G. T. Sheldahl. The following year, my son, Jeffrey, was born. My husband and I both continued working for Sheldahl in Northfield, but things would soon change.

The Vietnam War was raging at that time and my husband got drafted and was sent to Vietnam. During his absence, I became homesick for Germany and also wanted my parents to get to know their grandchild. I left my job, and flew to Germany where I went back to the job I held before coming to the United States.

My stay in Germany lasted only short of one year. I missed the friends I had made and the lifestyle to which I was accustomed. But most of all, I wanted to give my son a chance to grow up as an American. After all, he was an American citizen and I wanted to grant him that right.

After my son Jeff and I had returned to the US, we moved to the California bay area where my sponsors, Ed and Dorothy Cooper, lived. My husband and I had drifted apart and eventually divorced. I recall that period of time as very difficult. My son was still a toddler and needed the guidance from both parents so badly. Going to church was the best decision I made. There I found friends that were supportive of my situation and needless to say, I learned to hold my head up high and learn to walk the straight and narrow.

Soon, I began working for one of the Bay Area's largest newspapers. I loved the company, the people and my job.

It was 1969 when I received a telegram notifying me that my father had a severe stroke. He died a few days later at the age of 57 on September 3, 1969, which was my 25th birthday. My father had been through many ordeals in his life. It was very sad to have him taken from my mother and us at a relatively young age.

To our family, the memory of our father will always evoke thoughts of the many courageous deeds accomplished by this man. He took many risks to give his family a better life. My sister, brothers and I experience freedom today because he was so brave and courageous.

Sometime later, I applied for and obtained a position with a pharmaceutical firm in the Bay Area. It was a wonderful job and provided me, as a single mother, a comfortable living. There I met a cute French Moroccan secretary, who was a minister's wife. She convinced me to join a wonderful, singles ministry, where my son could also attend Sunday school classes. In a short time I had no doubt that her husband was one of the best and most beloved pastors in the Bay Area. His ministry provided me with the foundation for a lifelong commitment to Christ. This minister taught me so much of the wonderful aspects of our faith in God. He now has his own ministry called, "Free At Last."

The church offered a program called, "Big Brothers," which cared for children who were raised in single parent homes. We were once more walking in faith and things seemed to get better in my life.

My son Jeff grew up a handsome and intelligent young man. I am very proud of him. After graduating from high school he paid his own way through college. I did not have much saved in the way of funds, but he was willing to work and pay his own way. He graduated from the University of San Francisco with excellent grades. Today, he is married with three children.

In the meantime a wonderful position was offered to me by IBM, which I accepted. It provided me another wonderful opportunity. I had been single for 25 years and often prayed that God would send me a wonderful and lifelong companion. It took a long time but in 1989 I met Herb, who also worked for IBM. We fell in love shortly thereafter and were married in October, 1990.

While still dating Herb, my mother visited me at about the time we became engaged. She was happy that I was not going to be spending the rest of my life alone and she was especially happy that I had met a wonderful man.

My mom became very forgetful and for the last 13 years of her life suffered from Alzheimer's disease. We made several trips to visit her, but with each successive trip her cognitive powers were diminished. Eventually she no longer recognized me. She died at the age of 88, on December 22nd, 2002 in Germany. As noted on several occasions, she is and always will be my heroine.

My siblings and I are leading good lives and three of the four of us share in the American Dream and live in this country.

My older sister, Grete, lives in the state of Washington. Some years ago, her husband, Richard, died of cancer. She has remarried since. My brother Willie and his family live in Florida. My youngest brother, Alexander, remained in Germany and lives there with his two daughters. We stay connected by the internet. It is a wonderful invention, which permits us to stay close, while living far apart.

My husband Herb and I have been blessed with wonderful jobs and are enjoying life to the fullest in retirement in Roseville, California. We are involved in many activities. Several of my activities are due to my early love of art I had in elementary school. I work on websites as a hobby, decorate flowers at the church, and paint silk scarves and silk wall hangings whenever I can.

Herb and I have celebrated our 20th anniversary this year, 2010. After retiring we spent a few years in a large motor coach and traveled around this beautiful country of ours. In 2008, we gave up our nomadic life and purchased another home in Northern California.

I am eternally grateful to a gracious God for guiding my family and me through many difficult times, and most of all for the gift of life. He has led me back to the right path many times when I have strayed. I was blessed with a wonderful father and mother to whom this book is dedicated. They risked their lives often so we might have a better life.

Oh yes, I bet you are wondering what happened to mom's sewing machine. Her prize possession is now my night stand. I fall asleep every evening with it next to me. Sometimes I remember to put a few chocolates on it.

Hey Kids, Want Some Chocolates?

**Mother's sewing machine smuggled out
of Romania and East Germany**

About The Authors

Melitta Strandberg was born September 3, 1944. The story of her birth and subsequent events are a compelling story. Equally compelling are the quest of her parents to find freedom. They endured much to find a better life for their family. Their story began in Romania and is filled with many risks and many narrow escapes that could have ended their quest prematurely. Melitta's own quest for freedom ended before she was a year old, but those first few months of her life are intriguing and much about them remains a mystery. Thereafter she has led a successful and typical life. Her first 18 years were spent in Germany and the remainder of her life in the United States. Today she lives with her husband, Herb, in Northern California.

George E Pfautsch spent most of his working life as a financial executive with Potlatch Corporation, a major forest products and paper company. His final years with them were spent as the Senior Vice-President of Finance and Chief Financial Officer. Following his retirement, he began writing and speaking on the subjects of morality, justice and faith. He has published several books on those topics and he views this book as encompassing each of those subjects.

Edwards Brothers Malloy
Thorofare, NJ USA
January 17, 2017